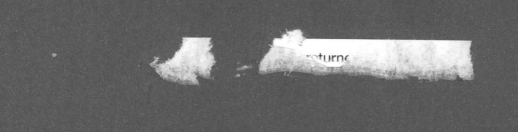

COULD AN OCTOPUS CLIMB A SKYSCRAPER?

...and other questions

Aleksei Bitskoff &
Camilla de la Bédoyère

QED Publishing

Octopuses are soft-bodied animals with eight arms.

They are cousins of slugs and snails.

Design: Duck Egg Blue
Editor: Ruth Symons
Editorial Director: Victoria Garrard
Art Director: Laura Roberts-Jensen

Copyright © QED Publishing 2014

First published in the UK in 2014 by
QED Publishing
A Quarto Group company
The Old Brewery
6 Blundell Street
London N7 9BH

www.qed-publishing.co.uk

A catalogue record for this book is available from the British Library.

ISBN 978 1 78171 583 3

Printed in China

Octopuses live in the ocean. These animals may look weird, but they are surprisingly smart.

Imagine if an octopus left the ocean to explore. Would she have fun?

What if an octopus went shoe shopping?

She would have to pick **four pairs** of shoes.

She uses her **eight arms** like legs to walk on the rocky seabed.

Sometimes, if an octopus
is in **danger**, she can
detach an arm.

Then she **grows** a new one.
But it would need a smaller shoe!

What if an octopus went to a fancy dress party?

She wouldn't need to shop for a costume.

She could just change her **colour** and **body shape**.

Under the sea, an octopus can pretend to be a snake, a rock or a fish.

But for a party, she could turn herself into
a **banana** or a **beach ball**.

She could even disappear by
blending in with her background -
that's a cool party trick!

Could an octopus play hide and seek?

"1, 2, 3, 4..."

She doesn't have any bones in her body, so she can hide in tiny spaces.

Octopuses hide under rocks or in small spaces when they want to rest. So she might doze off under the sofa!

What if an octopus went to the doctor?

The doctor would need **three** stethoscopes – one for each heart!

Octopuses need three hearts to pump their blue blood all around their body and arms.

Could an octopus climb a skyscraper?

An octopus could tackle
the hardest climb
without any
footholds.

Each of her arms is covered in up to 200 sticky suckers so she could walk right up the side of the building.

Under the sea, she uses her suckers to grab and grip slippery fish.

Could an octopus cook dinner?

She could use her **beaklike mouth** to open cans and her long arms to unscrew jars.

Under the sea, octopuses use their beaks to **drill holes** into shellfish or break them open.

They taste food just by touching it with their suckers.

Tonight's menu:

Raw fish
Raw crab
Slimy snails
Shellfish

What if an octopus played cards?

She would probably win!

She is very intelligent with a big brain in her head and a 'mini-brain' in each arm.

And she could play eight hands all at once!

What would an octopus do for pocket money?

She could wash cars with a **super-strong** jet of water.

An octopus can fire water from the

part of her body called a funnel!

The water shoots for several metres!

Would an octopus play in a sand pit?

She might dig a den in the sand.

She would use shells to decorate it.

And then she would lay her eggs in the den!
An octopus lays up to **20,000** tiny eggs at a time.

She looks after them for up to four months, until they are ready to hatch.

More about octopuses

Octopus is pointing to
the places where she lives.
Can you see where you live?

FACT FILE

Some octopuses are smaller than your
hand. Some octopuses are bigger than
a car. A common octopus like the one in
this book grows to be about 1 metre long.

Octopuses have eight arms. If an octopus
loses an arm it can grow a new one.

An octopus has a soft body, with no
bones. It can squeeze into tiny places
and it can change colour so no one
can see it.

Octopuses have three hearts and a
big brain.

Octopuses eat other animals, especially
shellfish. They hold onto their food using
the suckers on their arms.

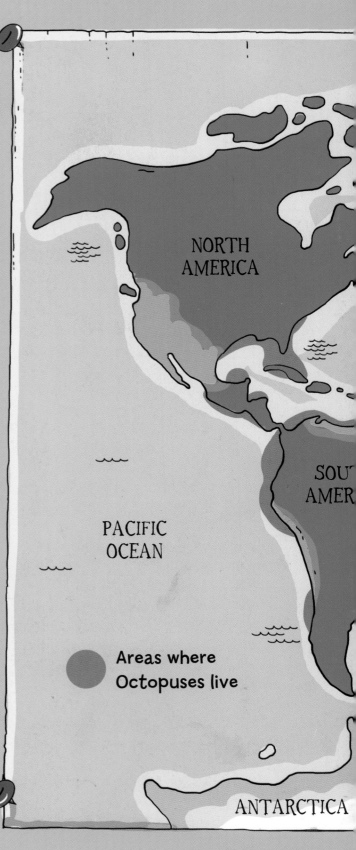

NORTH
AMERICA

SOUT
AMER

PACIFIC
OCEAN

Areas where
Octopuses live

ANTARCTICA

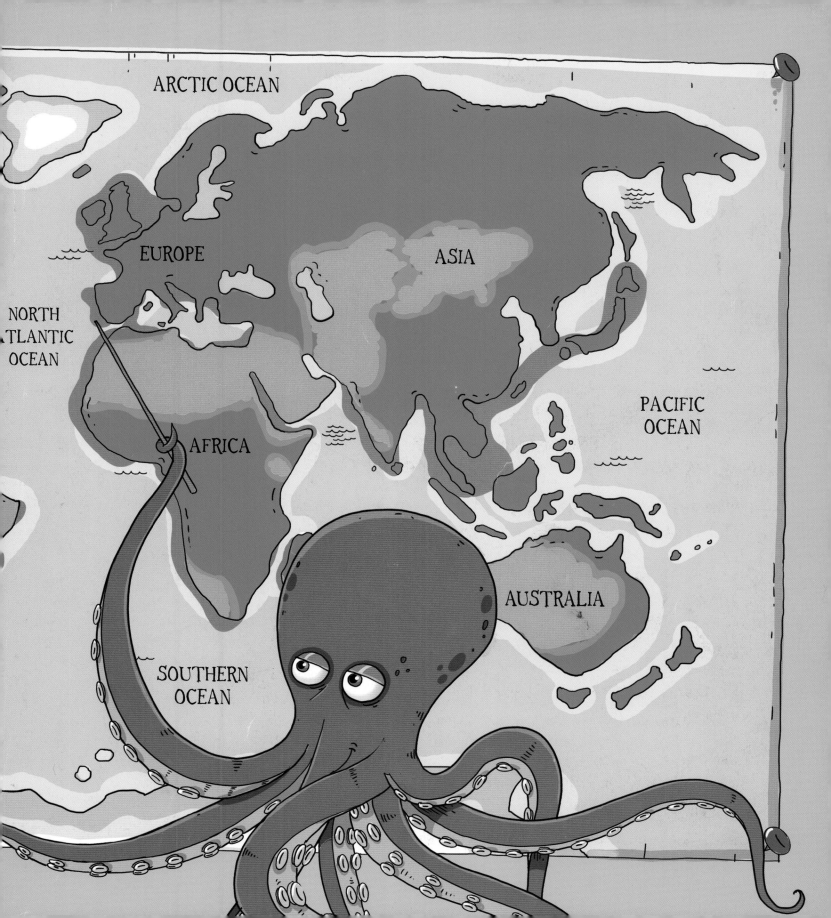

Greetings from the ocean!

POST CARD

I'm back in my cosy den, safe and sound, and nibbling on a tasty crab. I am keeping out of sight because there's a big shark swimming nearby! I've been playing tricks on him, pretending to be a banana – but he doesn't see the funny side.

Love, Octopus X

SENT BY OCTOPUS POST –
CAPE SAGRES, PORTUGAL

The Eaton Family
100 Bottesford Road
Nottingham
NG8 4RM
UK

234876356920323B734